Help! I'm Self-Employed...

Help! I'm Self-Employed...

Allan Rimmer

ISBN 978-1-4461-5632-2

Contents

A plain-talking, common-sense approach to increasing your business

You have my promise that you will definitely read through and finish this book inspired and with fresh, bright, new ideas for your business. No jargon, no gobbledygook. Just a plain-talking and common-sense approach to increasing the way your business operates for you. At the end of the day, you want to be doing more business where you are, don't you? Of course you do. If you're self-employed, an owner manager, a tradesperson, a shop owner, an arts or crafts professional, the messages in this book apply to you. Whether you're just starting out in business or you've been trading for a while, you're going to find a range of ideas in the following pages which will make your business that much more attractive to potential customers. And you're only going to read about inexpensive and low cost ideas and suggestions: that's my other promise to you!

Theory is fine and has its place but you'll find me a very practical man. In writing this book I've used actual lessons learned from my success in starting my own business from scratch; I've used actual lessons learned from growing my own and others' businesses; and I've drawn on my experiences gained along the way in sales, in marketing, in speaking to and giving workshops to many, many groups of entrepreneurs in the past few years. For you to get the most out of this book, I've also researched and prepared actual, real life examples of other businesses and what they've done, whenever and wherever I could.

At this moment, it may well be that you are only servicing a small percentage of those customers within your grasp. Maybe you're only scratching the surface of the number of customers who are out there but who either don't know you or don't know enough about you. Well, by the end of this book you'll have the inspiration, the ideas and the tools to help you dig a lot deeper below the surface. Once you've read it you should be able to reach a much, much larger percentage of customers, and just imagine what that might mean to you…

So… let's set the scene

What's in it for you? Why you should invest your time and read this book.

You know that there are more customers out there. They ought to be buying from you. You know they could or would buy from you, if only you could reach them; if only you could somehow get the right message across to them.

But, your brain says, wait – isn't this the province of marketing professionals? Something only big businesses do? You've heard about what they do and about how expensive they are. You've heard that what they do is complicated and that, after all, they are professionals like solicitors or chartered accountants, aren't they? Certainly the jargon they use is almost impenetrable; it's definitely confusing. The Plain English Society would surely have a field day with the literature put about by most marketing professionals. So, maybe you conclude that you'll never get past the gobbledygook, that you'll never understand enough about marketing, that you can't afford any and that you just can't do what it takes in this confusing area. Stop right there. Listen up.

You can do it.
You can do it.
You can do it.

That could be your mantra; the one you chant every day, going to your place of work.

In this book you will see how you can do it, the job of the marketing professional. And you'll see how to do it at the lowest possible cost as well. Don't be confused by the supposed might of marketing professionals; it's all a myth. Yes, that's right: a myth. They are no smarter than we are. We live in a world of practicalities, you and I. This world of ours existed long before the advent of marketing professionals.

They live in a world which is confusing, hard to penetrate and complex to the outsider, to the uninitiated.

I started out this introduction by stating that you know there are more customers out there, that they should be buying from you if only you could reach them and get the right message across. In the following chapters I'm going to expose the myth of the marketing professional and at the same time show you how to do it yourself. Together we'll cut through the jargon. We'll talk plainly and apply some straightforward common-sense so that you can reach more customers than you ever have before, and at the lowest possible cost.

ONE:

The end of the 'B' word

Are you, like me, sick and tired of trying to figure out what exactly branding means and what it means for your business? I reckon that this is the number one word employed by marketing professionals and PR firms to keep us in the dark. It's shrouded in some kind of mystery or haze and we can't quite see what it is. If you look up the definition in Wikipedia, the online, free encyclopedia, you see 'branding' defined:

… people distinguish the psychological aspect of a brand from the experiential aspect. The experiential aspect consists of the sum of all points of contact with the brand and is known as the brand experience. The psychological aspect, sometimes referred to as the brand image, is a symbolic construct created within the minds of people and consists of all the information and expectations associated with a product or service.

That, certainly, keeps me in the dark. What about you? Yes? Well, let today be the day that signals the end of the 'B' word!

Let's have no more 'brand experience'

No more 'brand image'

No more 'brand expectations'

Does anyone know what these things mean? NO !

Let me tell you about a well-known marketing consultancy, which is billed as 'an organisation specialising in the provision of branding, brand engagement and brand guidance'. They have offices around the world and hundreds of employees. 'Branding' is at the heart of everything they do. If you look on their website, you'll see this confusing statement: 'We have proven expertise in brand strategy, brand design and brand innovation. It's all about a unique fusion of strategy and creativity focused on unlocking value…'

What does it all mean? Do you think it's just so confusing? Are you, too, left in the dark on this topic?

Do you remember the story of The Post Office? In 2002, the good old Post Office, after 300 years of history, always known for being solid, established and reliable, overnight became known as Consignia. This was the fiasco of the new century. The name came about following a two-year branding project which ended with the dreadful nine letter word. According to BBC News Online at the time, the London consultancy which oversaw the project was, of course, fully aware that the Post Office was expanding internationally. However, the newspapers of the day tell us they went ahead and named it Consignia. This is all part of the myth surrounding what branding is. After this re-naming, it was discovered, that in every Spanish-speaking nation around the world, the word 'consignia' means 'lost luggage'! A great name for a delivery service, eh? Can you believe it? So, how expensive was the completion of that rebranding project? Answer: very.

Let's have no more 'brand engagement'
No more 'brand management'
No more 'brand innovation'
No more 'brand guidance'
No more 'brand strategy'
No more 'brand design'
No more 'brand plans'
No more 'brand equity'
No more 'brand vision'
No more 'brand metrics'
No more 'brand evaluation'
No more 'brand acquisition'
No more 'brand awareness'
No more 'brand enhancement'
No more 'brand communications'
No more 'employer brand attribution'

And, there are so many consultancies out there, that this terminology con-trick of the so-called marketing gurus is like an ever-multiplying organism.

Let's have no more 'brand propositions'
No more 'brand performance'
No more 'brand extensions'

No more ‘brand mapping’
No more ‘brand value’
No more ‘brand insistence’
No more ‘brand personality’
No more ‘brand planning frameworks’

And it goes on…

Let’s have no more ‘brand architecture’
No more ‘brand identity’
No more ‘brand style’
No more ‘brand literacy’
No more ‘brand situation analysis’

And while I’m having this rant I’m going to add one more word to our list…’synergy’. What on earth is that all about? Is this another word devised to keep us in the dark? If so, let’s definitely have no more synergy. There, now that that’s a banned word as well, I feel so-o-o much better!

Any more additions? If you come across any examples of this doublespeak, feel free to drop me an email and I’ll add your contribution, with an acknowledgement, to my website’s ever-growing list of banned words and phrases.

TWO:

Words we can and will use

Remember that I described myself as a practical man. Well, there are five practical words which I choose to use, and which I encourage you all to use: marketing, selling, promoting, image and reputation.

Marketing

'All the things you do to make the telephone ring.'

This is the definition that Harvard Business School gives to Marketing. It seems to me to be ever so simple; it's elementary enough for all of us to grasp easily. There may well be other definitions out there but this one I like well enough to pass on. And, what's more, ***You can do it.*** Marketing doesn't have to be a complex, confusing scientific discipline. It's largely about the application of common-sense.

I know that in a small or medium-sized business, time is at a premium. But do remember that marketing efforts are designed to get plenty of new customers coming in, lots of inactive customers coming back and all your current customers buying more. These results have to be your goals every day of every week, haven't they?

Those of you in charge are expected to be experts in everything: accounts, personnel, production, distribution, and so on. Most business owners and managers don't have the luxury of time. However, the effective application of marketing for business development is a great weapon to have in the armoury of any business, especially so for small or medium sized businesses.

Finding out about the markets open to you and ending up with a good understanding of those markets are the things you need to do.

To illustrate this, I always like to tell the classic story of the two shoe sales reps who were sent out to a desert island in order to investigate the market there and to end up with a good understanding of it. The island was inhabited by natives; in fact plenty of people lived there. After two days the first sales rep sent a text back to the Head Office saying, 'Bring me back home. This is hopeless; no one here even wears shoes.' The second sales rep sent a message back to Head Office saying, 'Send me supplies. You won't believe it but nobody yet wears shoes here!'

So which one of the two reps actually asked questions, would you guess? Finding out what potential customers think is the common-sense starting point of the things you need to do.

Speaking to your prospects and to your customers is the very best way of finding out:

- What type of person will buy from you?
- How many of each might he buy?
- What price would he consider good value?
- What else might complement your range?

This finding out about your market can be done over the telephone; it can be done chatting face to face; or, it can be done by the use of a questionnaire.

Whatever method you choose to use, finding out what your potential and current customers think will put you streets ahead of your competition. Remember the old adage: *the more you know: the more you grow.*

If you want to grow your business you can't do it merely by guesswork. You need to know things about your customers, and it's this knowing which will stand you in very good stead indeed.

Selling

'All the things you do after you pick up the phone.'

Here is another simple and straightforward definition from Harvard Business School. If, in the first instance, marketing is all about understanding your customer and your marketplace, then selling will surely be a much easier task because all the early groundwork has been laid.

To illustrate this definition, let me tell you the story surrounding the Aga Cooker we have in our kitchen at home. At the end of the summer last year we arranged for our Aga to be given its annual service. It's a gas fired cooker. We had the same engineer come to the house as we have over the past seven years, though I'd never met him before. Each year previously my wife had been the one at home when he called.

On the day in question I happened to be in, greeted him, made him a cuppa and wrote out the cheque at the end of his service. I was amazed that he never asked me any questions; not one. Here was a perfect opportunity for him to learn more about me, his customer; about his market place. For instance, he could have asked about how my gas boiler was usually serviced as well as the Aga, about servicing my gas fire, or servicing my radiators. He could have asked me where I bought those special cleaning fluids for the Aga or where I bought those special cleaning cloths.

He could have asked me about the particularly long Aga oven gloves which we have to buy periodically so we can safely reach into the back of the oven; or the oven trays, hot pads and mats we have to use.

While he was there, in essence he had already 'picked up the phone', from me the customer, and the opportunities for him were numerous. I would have answered any questions he asked. I would have told him anything he wanted to know and more besides. I would have bought from him some extras which complemented what he did, for sure. If only he had asked.

I want you all to get into the habit of constantly thinking about the extra opportunities which you might take; what would be useful for you to ask in order to understand your customer that much more? Just what are those extra or complementary things which might interest your customer, the next time you deliver to him your service or product?

Promoting

'The use of tools and techniques to keep customers reminded of you.'

Examples of these tools and techniques can be things such as offering free gifts or vouchers. Other examples could be about leaving your name and contact details, or information about other products or services which you supply, where the customer will come across them. Perhaps further examples could include providing certain guarantees or making customer competitions available.

The Aga man… What could he have done differently under the heading of 'promoting his business'? Apply common sense to this question and a number of answers leap at you from nowhere. How about:

- A label on the inside door of the Aga with his name and number on?
- Asking for my email address and promising to alert me prior to the next service due?
- Leaving me a business card or postcard, a leaflet or brochure, a pen with his number on, or all these?
- Taking pride in completing the service log book and putting his official stamp in it?
- Slipping an envelope through my door or contacting me three months prior to the service?

Image

'Your actual product or service, combined with what your customer expects from it.'

Your image is all about the impression made on your potential customers and others. Your image is the effect you have on someone who looks at you and your business but who perhaps doesn't yet know you.

Remember the saying: *You don't get a second chance to make a first impression.* When people look at you in the street, at your vehicle on the road, or at your shop front, what do they think? What image do you convey?

When your customers receive your product, how is it wrapped or boxed? Is it in an old cardboard box? Is it in a sharp-looking and customised package? How is it sealed? What exactly does it look like and what impression does it give? Do you include your product cards, leaflets or flyers? What about a note expressing a thankyou for the order? Any inserts or materials you attach to the order like this can become quite critical and will perhaps mean the difference between another order or not.

Reputation

'The views that your customers, or potential customers, hold about you.'

To have a reputation is to be known for something notable. Remember that a reputation can be a poor one as well as a good one.

In 1991 an estimated £500 million was wiped from the value of Gerald Ratner's jewellery company, according to *The Daily Telegraph,* after he had joked that Ratner's high street chain 'sold a pair of earrings for under a pound, which is cheaper than a sandwich from M & S, but probably wouldn't last as long.' He went on to say, in his address to the Institute of Directors, that a tacky sherry decanter they sold was so cheap because it was 'total crap.' The impact on the business' reputation was immense and is now a prime example of how a poor reputation can kill.

By contrast, Beaverbrooks the Jewellers, a family business, won *The Sunday Times* Best 100 Companies To Work For Awards in 2009. The newspaper reported:

… go into a Beaverbrooks' shop and you'll leave with an extra bit of sparkle in your life. By offering the weary shopper a cup of tea, a comfortable seat, a few minutes of chat and detailed advice about the products on offer, the company's staff are doing all they can to boost the buying experience, and put a smile on the face of shoppers.

What a reputation they have! A cuppa and a chat? When you have the right products or service, the rest is really all down to a common-sense approach, isn't it?

THREE:

Do you know who your customer really is?

Everything starts with your customers or potential customers. But just who exactly are they? If you run a business you may instinctively know that there are 'right' customers and 'wrong' customers.

At one time, it was reported, Marks and Spencer had lost the sense of who their customers were and what they wanted. In 2001 M&S began the process of recovering this apparently lost ground. They spent a whole year listening to customers, gathering a range of views on what was expected of a responsible retailer in the twenty-first century. Once they'd determined the issues, they also looked at peers and competitors, assessing how M&S performed comparatively on each issue. Then they made some commercial decisions, prioritising key factors such as the potential for M&S to achieve competitive advantage. In the food division alone, they apparently produced sixteen key issues and then spent another eight months working with the food business to embed those issues within a wider growth strategy. They were, of course, ultimately successful.

***You can do it*, and in a lot less time!**

If you can exactly identify a profile of your prospective customers, then the task of deciding what you want to know from them, how to approach them and how to sell to them becomes so much easier. Please don't be fooled into thinking that your customers can be anybody or everybody. If you take that approach then you are likely to end up selling to nobody. Try to think of it this way: jumping up and down in a small puddle is far more effective than trying to make a splash in a big ocean!

When you develop a profile of your customers, start out by asking yourself clarifying questions about those who, in theory, could buy from you. Are they male or female, old or young, members of a particular profession or occupation? Do they have a particular lifestyle or are they part of a group with common interests or special interests such as sports or hobbies? Do they own a particular type of house or live in a particular type of neighbourhood? Do they live within so many miles of here? Using the answers to these and any other questions you consider relevant, you can then start to figure out what it is they read, where they hang out, where they go and what they do?

If you provide business-to-business products or services, then your prospective customers aren't necessarily other companies! They could be the people who work at your customers' companies and who are perhaps responsible for ordering your type of product or service.

Once you've decided on your ideal customer profile or group, you now need to be absolutely clear about what they want, what they need and exactly what it is that you're going to offer them. Understanding this sort of thing will help you to develop the most effective type of marketing message to tell customers of the benefits of your product or service.

If you get this message wrong it's almost certain that your marketing efforts will fail and your customers will turn to your competitors instead; all because your product or service will have missed the target completely. You run the risk of wasting valuable time and money if you launch any marketing efforts before you've accurately identified your target customers and what they want.

So the very best thing you can do is to speak to some of your target customers first. And, of course, when you speak to a sample of your target customers you'll be testing your assumptions that the profile you've determined is the right one. You'll also be able to test your assumptions about what you think they want and why they should buy from you.

After you've accurately identified who your target customers are and what they want, your aim will then be to concentrate your marketing efforts, your sales efforts and your promotional efforts towards those who are the most likely to buy your product or service. It will now also become easier and less expensive to contact potential customers and you'll almost certainly face less competition.

Take, for example, the sole trader with his small gardening business, whose name is Sam. What Sam offered was grass cutting, pruning, clearing of leaves, tidying flowerbeds, general maintenance and so on, mainly to residential properties. He told me that two of his very best customers were ‘companies on the industrial estates outside the city.’ He’d been lucky enough to pick up one company on the recommendation from a friend and did a good job. Then the block of offices next door noticed him and he got their business too. But he also told me that although there were many large companies out there, he found the task of speaking to any of them quite daunting. Previously he’d only ever dealt with domestic properties for his gardening services and had never considered these commercial customers. Sam reckoned that dealing with any of the managers or directors at these companies and trying to get appointments and then sell his services to them was too difficult for him; that it was all too much.

We discussed this at length. We talked about his current two commercial customers and who exactly he dealt with at each one. We talked about how these businesses operated. I told Sam about how responsibilities would be divided at each company; in other words, the delegation of responsibilities. Eventually he came to understand that, typically, the decision to bring in someone to look after the lawns out front, was made by the front receptionist! So the profile of his customer wasn’t the big manufacturing company or the block of commercial offices: it was, typically, the humble receptionist; the type of person who maybe lived next door to him.

Once Sam had realised who his customer actually was, he understood why he’d had so much trouble previously. He’d been trying to speak to the wrong people and had wasted their time as well as his own. From that moment on, what Sam did was to approach all the front office receptionists and ask them, and no one else, how they managed any gardening requirements. Where had they gone for garden services in the past? How had the services been? He asked, if they had the chance how would they improve the services received? And so on. Sam always left his contact details and always asked for theirs. Needless to say, he moved his business forward in a much more structured way, and with much greater confidence than before. He now understood who his customers were, and he had gained specific information about what they were looking for.

Hot Tip! Make a list of all your current customers and divide the list into any obvious groupings. Write down a list of what each group wants or needs and see how they differ.

FOUR:

The least expensive (and most neglected) ways to advertise

Adverts in local newspapers and magazines

Only half of our spending on advertising works, the problem is that we don't know, we're not entirely sure, which half it is.

I don't know who originally made that observation but it does drive home a point: ads cost money and you could theoretically spend everything you have on adverts but still be uncertain of achieving the intended outcome. This is not an automatic and successful way of winning new orders.

For any small business with a small budget, advertising isn't usually the route to a sudden upturn in sales. It's important not to risk funds that your business can't afford on advertising schemes that can't guarantee a return. Prior thought is vital. If your headline doesn't capture the attention of readers right away, then you will not get the response you need. That means you'll lose profit.

Take notice of advertising going on around you and think of how you might adapt any to your business at some future point in time. Keep a file of advertising ideas you see from other businesses that you might adapt to use for yourself at some future time.

In particular, start a file of your competitors' advertising. Not to copy it, as that may confuse the customer, but do keep your competitors' ads over a period of time, to gain an insight into their thinking and what it is that's been said.

Look at your own trade press as well as that of other areas and industries. Whenever you see an idea that looks good, rush to the photocopier. Copy it immediately or you won't do it at all.

The structure of an advertisement.

If we're going to advertise then we should definitely do it right. The following tips will put you in the position of knowing the best way to design an advert.

The headline. Start with an eye-catching question. Words like *new, need, now, announcing, at last, how to, how, why, which, wanted, advice*.....these are words likely to capture attention.
Personalise headlines with *you* and *yours*. For example, 'When did your service engineer last call you?' Or, 'How can you fill your stationery cabinet without emptying your pockets?'

The body copy. This is the part that sells. Be honest but avoid phrases such as 'best deals in town'. Phrases like that merely serve to annoy people. Don't just list all the elements of your product or service and then expect that people will buy.

Call to action. In other words, always ask for the order, or get people to 'call now'. This will also help your advertising by giving the reader a reason to act straight away! Maybe include an incentive for people to call you.

You just have to look at examples of adverts in your local press to see those which have too many words, no questions posing a problem and even fewer suggesting the solution to a problem. The following examples have been taken from a local newspaper almost word for word, except that for copyright purposes and privacy I've amended any company names and numbers.

AAA PLUMBING COMPANY

All Plumbing and Gas Work Completed

- Mechanical Repairs
- Electrical Repairs
- Servicing Boilers
- Servicing Fires
- Installations
- Boiler Swaps
- Power Flushing
- System Upgrades
- Kitchens

Tel: 0113 289 7170

Mobile: 07979 815216

Computer Support and Advice

We Do It All

- Memory Upgrades
- Virus Removal
- Spyware Removal
- Advice & training
- Hardware Installations
- Software Installations

Call 0253-57899

Email: help@csa.co.uk

PENNINGTON-JONES
Employment Law Services Limited

Dismissal.......................Discrimination

Redundancy.....................Agreements

Non-Compete Clauses.........Tribunals

Appeals

We only deal with employment law for businesses and for individuals. We are specialist local solicitors.

Call us to discuss our expertise and to obtain some free FACT SHEETS.

Telephone: 01616 456789

The above examples show how not to compose an advert. There are too many lists of the services they offer. There are no questions at the outset to grab attention. There are no customer problems listed along with solutions provided.

Now look at the following examples of adverts which start with a question or statement and which are followed by a simple comment about how to solve the problem. Compare the two types and you'll soon begin to appreciate the difference between them.

Faulty Heating System?

Noisy Boiler?
Radiators Need Bleeding?
Radiators Hot/Water Cold?

We Can Fix It!

Call Richard Williams Central Heating Specialist
Telephone today on 01488 132456
Or 09780 217158

HAVE YOU MADE YOUR WILL?
Are you worried about what may happen to your estate? Do you want your family to be protected after you've gone?
We offer a professional service, in your own home, at a time to suit you and at an affordable price. *Please call 01411 – 345678* **WILLS EXTRA LEGAL SERVICES**

NEED MORE ROOM?
Running out of space in your home?
LOFT LADDERS Supplied and Fitted All work completed same day. For a FREE, friendly survey please contact us.
THE LOCAL LOFT LADDER COMPANY Telephone now on 07980 136566

Hot Tip! Start that file. Cut out and keep copies of any advertising ideas you see.

Hot Tip! Start a file of your competitors' adverts. Keep track of the quality and quantity of their ads and how much they spend.

Designing your own leaflets & flyers

Without a doubt it's tough out there. Everyone is battling for your customer's attention. And I mean everyone. Every time you send an email to a customer, so does someone else. Every time you send a letter to a customer, so does someone else. Whenever you offer your product or service, so does someone else.

Given that every year the population grows, as we know, (what are we up to now in the UK? Sixty million?), this is the sort of thing you're up against:

- 855 million books were sold in the UK in just 12 months.
- The average supermarket in the UK stocks over 50,000 lines.
- The average individual watches four hours of TV every day in the UK.

Everyone and everything is fighting for the attention of your customer. And I'll tell you what else...some of these statistics above are several years old.

You need to be different, you need to catch attention, and you need to be doing things in the right way only. Putting together leaflets and flyers is yet another simple and straightforward area that you can do for yourself without the need to spend a small fortune. But what's the difference between these two items?

A leaflet is a printed sheet (or sheets) which may be multi-sided or folded and is considered to be rather like an open letter. A flyer, generally considered to be a single sheet, is likely to be more directly to the point. You can have A4, A5 and A6 leaflets and flyers, A6 being the smallest. The reason promotional leaflets and flyers are small is so that they can be easily dispensed and distributed, and because they may only be looked at fleetingly, facts need to be kept to a minimum.

So, how on earth do you catch attention? How do you make your leaflets and flyers, whether hard copies or electronic copies, grab the attention that you want? One of the first principles is to focus on the type of customer you want, do not try to grab the attention of everybody or anybody. How many times I make that comment. First principles!

The second principle is never, never to underestimate the power your words have. You need, therefore, to be good at writing copy, or finding someone who is.

The third principle is to think in terms of weeks or a few months for the life of your flyer. Don't think that you can order thousands and have enough for next year as well.

Remember, variety is the spice of life.

The fourth and final principle here is to record and monitor the responses. Not all things will work all the time, as we know, but when you measure the responses and keep a record of what response came from where, well, then you can do more of what proves to be effective and less of what doesn't work. Simple, isn't it?

Rules for leaflets and flyers:

- Keep it simple. Try not to explain too much and keep your text short.
- If inserting into an envelope, consider using a coloured or a shaped envelope.
- Make the message on the leaflet easy to respond to; give a clear idea of what the reader is expected to do.
- Persuade the reader to take action.
- Use a time limit or close date.
- Do remember that variety is the spice of life.

Search Google for 'free leaflet design' and you'll find a list of companies that provide free tools and ready-made templates to use. You should be able to choose from literally hundreds of designs or even create your own. You'll then find it easy to add in your own text, your logo and so on. It will take you only minutes to put together and it's likely that you'll receive the finished product within a matter of days. The design may be free but you will have to pay for the printing of the leaflets or flyers. However, we are talking about a few pounds per thousand. For example, a budget, single-sided flyer might cost only £6.00 per thousand. Maybe you'll have to order a minimum of more than a thousand though. Higher quality, double-sided or folding leaflets might cost from around £50 per hundred. Just as with everything else it pays to shop around.

Hot Tip! Before signing off a leaflet or flyer to be printed, check, double check and triple check the content. It's much better to take the time out then rather than have to pay out for another print run later.

Designing your own product cards

Product cards, sometimes called postcards, are a great way to communicate. They are effective and efficient and they can generate awareness fast - and do remember: people keep postcards.

The key thing about product cards is the speed with which a potential customer can view your message. They measure 139mm x 107mm (that's 4 ½" x 8 ¼" in real money). On the front of the card, of course, should be your key advertising message, while on the back will be how the customer can get in touch with you or respond to you.

This is the time to use full-colour printing on heavy card stock. As with logos, business cards, flyers and leaflets, you can tap into literally thousands of template designs available from suppliers. You could also upload your own photos or logo to help with the design

You can be imaginative; you can use the same style as you do in advertising; and in fact you can use the same advertising layout, except now it's a lot more colourful.

Do they cost much? Again, if you were to Google 'free postcards', you may well hit on a choice of ten to twenty-five free cards. For a print of 100 it may cost about £10.00. Yet again, it's always worth shopping around and comparing prices.

Because these cost more than other items we've already discussed, my recommendation is to distribute only to specific individuals. Give to people who are thinking seriously about buying from you, or give to those who could well influence the buying behaviour of others.

Hot Tip! Use a digital camera to take photos of your finished products. Build up a small library of single items or groups of items and ask others what they think of the photos, using only the best on your product card.

Signage boards are it!

Putting out a sandwich board or similar will always attract the attention of passers-by: people almost always look at them. Yet, as I drive through housing estates or around industrial or commercial estates, I always see so many lost opportunities. When I refer to 'lost opportunities' I'm also actually thinking about those appalling signage boards which are visible in so many places. They may point to a business in a tacky way or simply overflow with too much information. A bad-looking signage board is more likely to put people off than entice them and I've seen some horrible ones, some very embarrassing ones, in my time.

If you're to display yourself in a positive way, in an appealing way, then do so with a little thought. Signage boards can work wonders for you and there's no doubt about it: people know you're there. Your name is continually noticed; you become a regular part of the local landscape. Without it no one knows your name.

The only thing which is worse than a tacky signage board is having no board at all. Why is it that tradespeople who carry out work at their customer's location, whether a house or office, ignore this method of broadcasting, this way of announcing their presence? If I had a message to pass on to every painter and decorator, every service engineer, every electrician, car valeter, plumber, gas fitter, gardener, interior designer, carpet layer, carpet cleaner… it would be this: don't ignore the strong possibility that any neighbour or passer-by, seeing your signage board, will think to himself, 'Well, if he's good enough to do a job at that location then that's a good enough recommendation for me. I'll call him.' Or, 'I've always wondered where to find a good… Obviously he's good, or he wouldn't be there.'

You can have a signage board for next to no cost. When you compare the amount you might spend in a newspaper with the potential in having this 'advert' outside your place of work there is no contest. You can get an A-Board, a D-Board, a Pavement Board, a Chalk Board, a Breezer Board, Swing Board or even a Lawn Sign. The choice is immense and the cost very low, starting at maybe £8.00. You can have high-impact on-street advertising, and of course you can have print on both sides for a few extra pounds.

You can also have a magnetic vehicle sign which is ideal for temporary applications and shared (business / private) vehicles. Just about any design can be applied to the magnetic sign surface, from simple text layouts to full-colour photo images. Yet again, everyone who walks past where you're working that day will know that you're there and what your services are.

Hot Tip! Just like your other printed materials, give a little thought. Apply some common sense to this subject, and remember to keep it simple.

Hot Tip! Don't have too much text.

Hot Tip! Consider whether people will see your sign board close up or from a distance and choose your letter size accordingly.

Press Releases: a no-cost way to advertise

If you want free advertising for your business, then the most effective way is to write a press release. **You can do it!** You can have these published in your local press, in magazines or on the internet.

If you think about it, any story about your business is likely to be more widely read and more likely to be believed than an advertisement which people know you've paid for. You immediately become more credible, and the publicity that a news story can generate will directly contribute to enhancing your image and reputation; something which otherwise might have cost you a small fortune.

Be assured that journalists are always on the lookout for a story that will appeal to their readers.

So, where would you send your story, your press release, if you had one? Start by phoning your target publication and getting the name of the journalist responsible for your topic or geographic area. Find their email address as well. You could go to a media directory or go to a trade publication to find the publication you want. Just Google 'media directory' or 'trade publications directory'; you'll be amazed at what you'll find.

You could publish your press release on the Internet; it's a great way of publicising your website and your business generally. It can certainly help to increase the flow of traffic to your website. Simply Google 'free internet press release'; you'll find a variety of sources to help you in your quest.

How to prepare your press release.

It's always important to grab attention immediately with an eye-catching headline. If you then proceed to write about something unusual, revealing or different you'll keep that attention. Local newspapers like to focus on local news, so in the first lines of your press release try to quote the town name.

Other ideas that might help are as follows: a charitable connection or sponsorship of a project; a customer survey that has unusual findings; details about an unusual customer or job you've just done; you or your business winning an award. These are all about people and are what's known as 'human interest' stories. Take a look in your local press to see the variety of human interest angles already employed. This will certainly give you a good idea of the angles used and styles of story.

A press release should really be no more than a page long and will be perhaps no more than 500 to 700 words. If you're writing a press release for the internet, these are generally much shorter, just 300 or 400 words long. Write it in short paragraphs. Wherever possible you should try to include a photograph: a picture paints a thousand words, and all that…

For your guidance, you could write about any of these ideas to get you started:

- The team you sponsored in a local charity fun run.
- The new contracts you've just won.
- A customer who saved money through using your services.
- The results of your latest customer opinion survey.
- The launch of a new product.
- How your service somehow relates to the World Cup, or Mothers' Day or Christmas…

Or how about releases that focus on hints and tips:

- Ten ways to reduce your heating bills.
- The best way to bake the perfect pie.
- Five ways to conserve water and help the Environment.

Hot Tip! Make use of the press release template I've included in the appendix at the back of this book

Hot Tip! Don't exaggerate. Don't use too many 'fantastics' or 'fabulouses'.

Hot Tip! Get someone to check it through before you send it off, for spelling mistakes and readability.

Hot Tip! Local is good! Don't think you have to aim for *The Sunday Times* business section.

Hot Tip! Practise writing a good press release and see how easy it is. At no cost, post or email your release to a large number of local news outlets.

Hot Tip! Build your list of journalists. Buy newspapers, pick up free magazines and check out local community organisations and websites.

FIVE:

It's never too late to start out right

Business logos – do you need one?

Yes! Your company logo can obviously have a significant impact on how your business is perceived. This impact can, of course, be either positive or negative, so a good logo design should be memorable and help to reinforce the message you want your customers to get. You want people to look at your logo design and see just what your company stands for.

But do you need to approach expensive professionals to put a logo together for you? If you think that these professionals are the only ones able to design a logo and that a logo is out of your reach then definitely read on.

According to an article in *The Times* newspaper in 2009, a redesign of the NHS logo was commissioned by the Department of Health to raise awareness of the 60th anniversary of the NHS. Ministers contracted with a commercial design firm to conceptualise and update the NHS logo for this anniversary. According to the article, a creative director and senior designer at the firm took ten days designing the figure 60 next to the usual NHS emblem, charging £6,000 a digit. Total cost for this new logo was £12,000. You can hardly believe it, can you?

The logo below is not meant to be an exact duplicate of the original, but simply something resembling it, in order to give you an idea of how the logo evolved from *NHS* to *NHS60.*

NHS 60

The article in *The Times* went on to say that government department spending included £153,522 on branding and logos to launch FERA, an agency that inspects plants and bees, and a £21,090 rebrand that changed the colours of the government's HomeBuy programme logo only months before one of its key schemes ran out of money.

Well, you can rest easy because I can show you how you can make your own logo. Yes! **You can do it** and do it for free!

All you have to do is search Google for 'free logo design' and you'll get a list of free logo-maker tools. Some are really basic and quite standard while others can be more sophisticated and include a catch that means you have to link the logo back to them for printing onto their products. The design of a good logo can be an art form in itself but it's also something which you can easily do on your own. When using a free design tool you should be able very easily to insert any numbers or text you want and include an icon or symbol from a library of symbols. You should easily be able to amend the font to your liking, add colour where you want it and then polish everything off with some additional design options.

The following five simple points to watch out for should guide you through this design stage:

- Keep It Simple. I know that I keep saying this but, it's so easy to do too much, to try to be too elaborate, when simple is best.
- Use two colours only. Especially when you are starting out and you're trying to keep costs to a minimum, using only two colours is much more reasonable in cost than printing in

full colour. There will also be more impact with just two colours and you can still look professional. Remember that the colour you finally decide on will help to form an image of your company. Green is easily associated with an environmentally conscious company; pink with a very feminine company; red is strong and aggressive; yellow can be seen as associated with children or sunshine.

- Keep it in proportion. Remember that your logo may be used in many different ways, such as on adverts, business cards, postcards, letterheads, flyers and so on. Don't let your logo be too long or too short.
- Keep the font easy to read. Don't be too elaborate; this is an easy trap to fall into for those new to this sort of design. Fonts which are too fancy can be hard to read. Remember your customers and make the reading easy for them.
- Be different from the competition. Your logo should be obviously different from that of the competition and, as far as possible, unique.

Look at some well-known logos such as *McDonald's, Apple* or *Nike*. These three logos are often seen as symbols only; no words. However, you instantly recognise each one. If you're lucky enough to find a relevant symbol for your own logo, then of course use it.

For other classic examples of using the name of the business itself as an integral part of the logo just look at Virgin, Google or Ebay. For you and me, this is a much more straightforward way to design a logo.

Hot Tip! Take your business name and try your hand at logo design using the free software I mentioned.

Hot Tip! Look at the logos of your competitors. Rate each on a scale of 1 to 10, 10 being the best. Decide what it is that makes the best ones stand out so much.

Business names – create the right impression

Choosing a name for your business can be fun. You also need to get it right for the simple fact that your business name creates an impression and customers may infer a lot from it. It's how you answer the phone; it's how your customers perceive you. So take an objective approach and look at this through your customers' eyes.

Your business name is going to appear everywhere: in Yellow Pages, other business directories, your website, business cards, letterheads, compliment slips, advertisements, uniforms and so on. What should you consider when deciding on a name for your business?

Firstly, is it a good idea to include your own name? The real question here might be, 'How well known are you in the community?' If you are well known then use that familiarity with your name to good effect. If you're not well known then why not choose another approach?

Maybe the name should reflect what your business does; cleaning, selling, building, servicing, consulting? How about these three plumbing businesses that offer exactly the same services?

J G Richardson & Son Ltd.
Star Services
HomeSafe Plumbing.
Which do you think is the best name?

How about these painters & decorators?
M J Donaldson & Co Ltd.
MJD Property Services
Rainbow Decorators
Which name do you think is the most appealing?

How about the bookkeepers:
Bailey & Co.
J B Business Services
Smart Price Bookkeepers
Which is the best here?

Some other very specific examples of current businesses using the trade or product in their names:
Alison's Carpet Care (carpet cleaning)
Hygiene Cleaning Services (household cleaners)
British Hairways (hairdressing salon)
Computer Doctor (computer repairs)
In The Dog House (dog trainer).
Avoid long and strange names. I mentioned earlier how it might appear in directories like the Yellow Pages where all entries are alphabetical.

Should you use the name of your city or town? Is that where your focus is?
For example…
Welland Valley Electrical Services
Leicester House Clearance
Stafford Garage Doors Ltd.

Do you need to sound traditional? How about **Churchill Accountancy Services**?
What about old fashioned? **Gentleman's Emporium** (clothing store);
How about young and trendy?
Kreativelook (hair salon);

Perhaps a more abstract name might suit?
Sole To Soul (holistic & beauty consultant)
Blooming Fresh (florist)
Change of a Dress (dress agency)
From Here To Maternity (maternity clothing & supplies)
The Bitter End (off-licence)
The Nutty Tarts (foods and gifts)
The Cod Father (fish & chips)
Blazing Saddles (bicycles)
All Screwed Up (nuts & bolts).
Choose the name to create the impression you want to convey.

Sole traders and partnerships can and should check whether the business name you want is already in use or not. Check in local directories, the phone book and the internet. If someone at the other end of the country is using the name you want, it should be ok; simply carry on and use that name. If a national firm is using it then you should choose another. If you really want to protect your trading name, a belt and braces job, then find out whether the name already has a trademark on it. Check out the Intellectual Property Office website to see whether a trademark has already been registered against the name you want. You can search the Trade Marks database free of charge at any time at www.ipo.gov.uk For you to take out your own trademark against your trading name is something you can do online and may well cost a couple of hundred pounds and more.

Choosing the name can be fun, but when it's done in a careful and considered manner the right name can be one of your biggest assets.

Don't forget to check that the domain name for your website is available too. Wouldn't it be just awful if you went to all the trouble of setting up with the trading name that you want only to discover that the domain name is not available? You can check for available domain names at www.nominet.org.uk which is an organisation set up to maintain a register of domain names and is the official registry of UK domain names. Do this at the same time as your directory search of trading names.

I read somewhere that Nick Jenkins, the owner of Moonpig greetings cards, apparently sat armed with a multitude of name combinations and only after a four day period finally declared and nailed the name he wanted and which was available, as both a domain name and a trading name: Moonpig.Com.

If you have decided to form a limited company then you must register your name with Companies House. There are some rules about the words you can and cannot use for your company name, and perhaps you should check those rules first of all. Go to www.companieshouse.gov.uk Do check that the name you have in mind for your limited company isn't the same or too similar to another name which is already registered. You don't have to do this but it could save any hassle later on as well as your time.

Finally, do remember that you are allowed to have more than one trading name! This does mean that you can have different trading names to see which provokes the biggest response and that could be very useful to you indeed. At the end of the year it is the limited company or you as the sole trader, who will have to submit an annual return and not the trading name.

Hot Tip! To get you started on selecting a business name, write down three names that reflect what your business actually does. Write down three names that make you sound traditional. Write down three names that make you sound young and trendy. Write down three names that make you sound modern and full of energy and ideas.

Use slogans to convey your memorable message

Everyone hears about those great slogans used by larger companies, usually those with money to burn on advertising and promotion. But there is absolutely every reason why you as a smaller business can use a slogan to help with your image. It could be to help with the perception of your business, or to help with your growth as a business. It's all about conveying a message which is memorable, short and catchy. You might use the slogan in your advertising, on your business cards, website, or stationery. You might even use it on any corporate work wear, in order to make you memorable.

Have a look at any slogan that may be used by a competitor; obviously you want to be different. An effective slogan ought to be brief; it ought to reflect just what your business is about. Remember that whatever you put into your slogan, such as a promise for instance, you'll then need to live up to that promise for as long as the slogan is around.

Using quantities in your slogan can be quite effective, but if this is a quantity with a promise, then you'll need to live up to it.

If you come up with a slogan that focuses on the wrong things, you might end up looking slightly foolish. It's important to get it right.

We all tend to remember humorous comments. How about a slogan with humour in it?

Slogans can certainly be inexpensive, especially for smaller businesses, and can work well to give you the sort of image you really want.

How to come up with a slogan.

Make a list of the benefits to a customer of your product or service. Decide on the top benefit. Using your top benefit, write down words that are related to it. Why not make use of a Thesaurus to help you? A Thesaurus is a book or special dictionary which contains lists of related words, topics and meanings. Come up with as many words as you can that relate to the benefit you've identified.

Once you have a comprehensive list, narrow it down to ten or so and then start playing around with the words. Try adding an active verb perhaps. See how creative you can be. Write every one down; don't leave any out because you might need that one as inspiration later. Finally, test them out on others. Don't just go with your own gut feeling. Ask friends and family what they think.

How about these which I've seen? Do you think they convey the right image?

Taxi

Our business is picking up!

Builders

Our reputation is building

Carpet Cleaner

Red carpet treatment for all

Cattery

So great 8 out of 10 cats prefur it

Cloth Finishers & Dyers

We Live to Dye

Catering

We cater to your needs

DIY Builders

We repair what your husband fixed

Taxidermist

We really know our stuff

Radiator Business

Best place in town to take a leak

Plasterer

Let's get plastered

Window Repairer

We can cure your window panes!

Flooring Business

We've got you covered

Hot Tip! For some zany ideas you might try Googling 'free slogan generator'. Enter one or more of your keywords and see how slogans are automatically conjured up from an online generator.

Business cards – don't leave home without one

Never, never, never be without one. You simply do not know who you're going to bump into out there. Whether you're on personal time or on business time, that one day when you have no business cards with you is the day that you'll meet the prospect you've been looking for. Guaranteed!

If you want one or two hundred free business cards you can simply Google 'free business cards' to find them. Hard to believe, isn't it? You will have to pay several pounds for delivery and that's all. You may get the printer's name on the back of each card but if you pay a few pounds more you can instead have a reverse to each card. It's all still incredibly cheap for you. My suggestion is to pay a little more; get some good quality card, not the cheapest. We want customers who tend to throw away the business cards of others, to keep yours instead. So think carefully about what image the front of the card portrays.

Think carefully too, about what you could have on the back of your card! Yes, let's use the back as well. You can list some extra comments about your products or services and how you can help your customer. But keep your message simple. One way to ensure your customers keep hold of your card until they need it is to include information on the back which they might refer to from time to time.

I've heard of all the following 'on the backs' which might serve to give you some inspiration:

- The carpenter who listed drill types
- The fruit and veg market stall owner's list of weights and measures
- The hairdresser's complimentary colour chart
- The gas fitter's energy saving tips
- The car mechanic's car accident procedures
- The complementary therapist's signs of the zodiac.

Alternatively, how about blank lines ready for a handwritten comment at the end of a meeting?

How about a nail or screw sizes chart?

Do remember that the whole idea is to catch attention and then to encourage the customer to actually keep your card, whether it's out of interest or out of necessity.

Hot Tip! If you are on good terms with your local pub landlord, restaurant owner, social club manager or similar, would they do you a favour and let you leave your business cards in a prominent position for people to take?

Hot Tip! Staple a business card to each invoice or receipt you issue. This means that customers will always know where to look when they next need your number.

Hot Tip! If you have a retail operation, craft stall, market stall or similar then keep a box of business cards by the till so that customers can easily pick one up and keep it in their wallet or handbag.

SIX:

Once you've got 'em, keep 'em (It's hard enough to win customers in the first place)

Be creative – have a competition

If you want to be really creative in your marketing efforts then carefully consider running business promotion competitions. As well as increasing the sales of your products or services to keep current customers interested, who knows, you might even have a bit of fun along the way! You can also use a competition to generate lists of other potential customers and prospects and it is one of the easiest and most cost effective ways to quickly build your database. I'm not suggesting something huge and costly but I am suggesting something more local and lighthearted.

In the 1990s the company Hoover gave away free flights as part of a promotional competition or campaign. According to the BBC, as a marketing exercise it may have been flawed from the outset. The public thought this promotion was too good to be true. Many Hoover customers discovered it was. Originally intended to shift a backlog of vacuum cleaners and washing machines, it ended up costing the company £48 million and dragging their name through the dirt. It was all too generous. Spend £100 on any Hoover product and two free, return flights could be yours. The marketing and PR individuals engaged in this fiasco were all professionals, of course, but still it went down in history as one of the greatest marketing disasters of all time.

Yet, *You can do it.*

Customer competitions may also sometimes be called business promotion competitions but they operate in the same manner. In a local and lighthearted way, the cost of entry should always be free and the prize you offer should be your very own product or service which is, of course, a negligible cost to you.

People who enter a competition are fully aware of the fact that they'll need to provide some information about themselves to you. This is your ideal opportunity to do a bit of customer data collecting. Also, people who enter a competition usually provide legible and accurate information, because they want to win! For you it could be as straightforward as collecting names and addresses. However, if you were to add just a couple more questions then you could really start to get an understanding of what your customers want.

How about the painter & decorator who awards the prize of a free room painting (of one small room) in exchange for an answer to, 'Are you planning on buying another house or selling your current home in the next twelve months?' Anyone who answers, 'Yes' will be likely to need some painting and decorating done either before they put their house up for sale or after they've bought their new one.

Alternatively, you could simply offer a family ticket to a theme park or similar. You'll need to include some basic terms & conditions in print for people to see. These can be very straightforward:

- *The competition winner will be picked at random*
- *The competition winner will be informed by... [dd/mm/yyyy]*
- *By entering this competition you agree to receive marketing information in the future. You will, of course, have the option to remove yourself from the contact list at anytime.*

You should include any restrictions such as age. Do include correct details of the prize and closing date. Do have an independent person supervise the draw.

All in all, make your competition fair, equitable and transparent.

Hot Tip! A competition can also be a way to attract some extra publicity for your business. Approach your local newspaper and give them your press release about the competition or, indeed, about the winner. Get the winner to say a few words that you can publish. Take their photograph.

Hot Tip! Remember that all entrants to your competition are a possible customer in the future. Even if they lose you should treat them with respect and keep them informed about the results.

Use testimonials and let your customers sell for you

If a potential customer has the slightest doubt about your product or service, then he is much more likely to be convinced by a third party; someone who is independent, a neutral person. Let your current customers sell for you by getting them to tell your potential customers how brilliant you are!

In order to understand clearly the power of testimonials you should look at this topic from the potential customer's point of view. Get inside the mind of your potential customer and you'll see that he's thinking: 'Can I trust you? You have to prove to me that you're good enough to do business with. I'm sceptical because I've had bad experiences before. When I've bought things in the past they haven't always lived up to the image I've been given…'

Certainly you can read stuff in the newspapers every day of the week about misrepresentation, about dishonest traders. There are TV shows devoted to the topic, just think about *Builders From Hell, Watchdog, Cowboy Builders* or *Rogue Traders.* People don't want to lose money or be cheated or caught out in some way. The job of a testimonial is to eliminate this big concern, this fear that people have. Remember that if you tell people that you're really good at what you do, people will ignore you, but when another person, a neutral third party says it, then it becomes much more like fact.

You can't just sit back, by the way, and hope a customer will write a testimonial out of the blue for you. You have to ask. Whenever you do a good job for a customer and he makes a complimentary comment, ask right there and then, if he would write those same comments down as a letter to you, and if you may use it to show other possible customers? Or you might, on a regular basis, ask customers for testimonials. There's nothing worse than seeing the same old one rolled out that was written back in 1988…

You have to ask, but more often than not customers are impressed that you've asked. They are usually quite happy to put something together saying what a good job you did. This is definitely one of the most powerful sales tools you have. If you are just starting out in business, one of the biggest hurdles you might face is that of credibility, or lack of. You don't have a huge track record of success as yet, but you still need to convince any potential customers who might be uncertain. Written testimonials will make sure that you are convincing and will close any credibility gaps which exist.

If the first rule of testimonials is to ask, the second rule must surely be to resist the temptation to rephrase your customer's words. If you do rephrase you could well reduce any 'believability' factor. Finally, wherever possible use a photograph. If you can print a photo of the customer or a photo of the completed job, or before and after photos, where appropriate, you'll hugely increase the power of the testimonial.

As a final word on the subject, don't be shy. People will always be happy that you're asking for a testimonial. At worst they may be too busy just at the moment; at best you'll have the proof you need to win over your next customer!

In the Appendix at the back of this book I've included an example of a testimonial form. Feel free to copy this form or amend it in any way. Any time spent capturing a comment from your happiest customers will be productive time spent indeed.

Hot Tip! Why not, after receiving payment, give your customer a thank you call and ask for the testimonial during that follow-up?

Lapsed customers – a good way to a fast increase in sales

Although continually acquiring new customers is important for growth, staying in contact with previous customers is a straightforward and cost-effective way to keep your customer base growing. Customers who have dealt with you before but who may not have dealt with you recently, are your lapsed customers. They may, for a whole host of reasons, not have had any contact with you for some time. The average business in the UK loses, at a minimum, 20% of its customers every year. For many businesses customer losses are even higher, yet very little is usually done to win back those lost or lapsed customers. Of course, if you do nothing then nothing will happen; but what is the 'something' you can do?

If you were to ask other businesses how often they contact lapsed customers, the answer is likely to be that they rarely, if ever, do so. The reason is that these customers are considered to be at the end of their life with no hope of revival. However, the odds are very favourable indeed for successfully winning them back and turning them into active customers once again.

The problem about lapsed customers is that they are almost certainly buying elsewhere, though you're not aware of it. I know from personal experience how easy it is to be so busy that you don't notice when they're gone. And at what point do you finally conclude that you have lost them? You have to decide how long that period is. Maybe it's months; maybe it's longer.

What should you do? Simply phone them up. Don't write to them and don't email them if you can possibly avoid it. Maybe you can't avoid it; it's just that the personal call can reap much greater benefits. You could say, 'It's been a while since we did business with you. Have we upset you or let you down in any way?' You'd be surprised at how many people will respond in a positive way. The response may well be, 'Oh no, we hadn't forgotten you.' The chances are that they had, of course, but you need to allow them to save face. So let them do that and then take their very next order. Of course there could well be a complaint hidden in this group. If so, welcome it. Learn from it. Promise to rectify it. Win some new support. Perhaps you'd never ever know what's upset them unless you simply asked.

Lapsed customers like this can be a good way to a fast increase in your sales, in your profits. From today onwards, set up a project so that you automatically contact them once your preferred time period has been passed.

Hot Tip! As soon as you make a sale or complete a job for your customer, enter their contact details into your diary, so many months ahead, as a reminder, to suit you.

Hot Tip! Get into the habit: establish a system to contact lapsed customers; leave no stone unturned.

What do they think of you? - getting customer feedback

Do you really know what your customers think or where your customers are coming from? Do you know what industry sector they're in or what type of people they are? Do you know what interests them or what their ideas are?

If you want to improve or expand your business then one of the best ways to start is to get feedback from your customers. Try to imagine how powerful the answers to these questions are. If knowledge is power, then by gaining this knowledge you could become powerful indeed.

The more you know about your customers and about what they like or dislike, their favourite colours, why they buy from you and so on, then the more you'll be able to target and win over new ones. Questionnaires and surveys can help you to get those answers.

You might want to ask your current customers where they think you can improve. With a simple questionnaire you can also ask current customers about other products they might like. ***You can do it!*** You can ask them about your deliveries, your location and about areas to improve your service.

Do have a look in the Appendix at the back of this book to see a sample customer feedback form you could use. Feel free to copy this or amend it to suit and use it any time.

Think about giving each customer a small gift for completing the questionnaire. How about giving them a free pen, a notepad, or a key ring? Give them something with your name and phone number on, of course.

Finally, do this on a regular basis - maybe a couple of times each year. Take the opportunity to tell your customers that you are interested in what they have to say and in their opinions. Just doing that in itself might make all the difference in the world in which they live. Remember that customers like to offer an opinion. Tell them that you're interested in what they have to say.

Hot Tip! Why not attach a customer feedback form to each invoice you send out?

Hot Tip! Compile the results every quarter and use these facts as part of a press release.

Reward your customers with a loyalty scheme

Most of the content of this book has been about winning new customers, or it's been about winning back lapsed customers. The efforts we go to are huge in these areas and so they highlight just how important it is to keep the customers we already have and to keep them happy. Whatever the cost is to your business of attracting a typical, new customer, well this investment would be entirely lost if they then leave you and go to a competitor.

When you start to work out just how much profit you get from your best customer in a year, and then multiply that by the next five years or longer, it's huge, isn't it? Yet that total could also be your potential loss if the customer goes elsewhere. A key method of avoiding that scenario is to initiate a customer loyalty scheme.

A typical scheme needs to reward customers once they have reached a certain level of business with you. Any scheme which rewards loyalty and goes on to extend the purchasing life of the customer has got to be a good one. Ideally, the benefit which you give to your customers in your loyalty scheme should be redeemable against your own products or your own services. The customers stay happy because they get something for a lower cost: you stay happy because the cost isn't that much to you. What you'll need to do is to strike the balance between the potential loss of your full-priced business profit and the potential gain of extending customer relationships.

So how do you devise such a scheme? The first part of the answer is by making sure that you set the level of spending by your customers (the level at which you'll also reward them) as higher than the average level spent by your average customer.

You could have the type of scheme whereby you 'stamp' a square on a card for every £*x* spent. When there are '*y*' stamps you then give the reward. People do like to watch things grow and perhaps this method is relevant to your customers.

A more straightforward scheme might be to offer a discount on the next purchase, once a certain spending level has been reached. Alternatively, you could invite your customers to a special event as a way of rewarding their loyalty. How about a wine and cheese evening, or a bacon butty and coffee morning? You could have special offers available at such events as well.

You could send out thank-you notes to your customers or even send birthday cards as a way of paying attention to them; perhaps anniversary cards for one year after their purchase?

Finally, you should remember that a certain number of your customers will be lost each year, and for a wide variety of reasons. A good loyalty scheme is one way of reducing the average numbers lost. It's also a fact that sometimes customers are lost because of a lack of attention from you. Keep in contact! Anything which will extend a customer's life with you has to be a priority. The best scheme, of course, may be to simply continue providing a first class service to your customers!

Hot Tip! Take your five largest, most regular customers and work out just how much they're worth to you in a five year period. Staggering, isn't it?

SEVEN:

Don't die, when facing an audience

The first rule of networking is – don't sell!

Networking lunches, networking breakfasts, networking evening meetings. We hear about them all the time, from chamber of commerce-type events to private, commercial networking businesses. What's important if you intend to go to an arranged event is to choose the right one. Look ahead of time; are they your type of people? Ask yourself whether you will benefit directly from getting to know any of the people who are attending this event.

The alternative to arranged events is when you meet at other gatherings where the purpose for being there is not primarily to network but may be something else entirely. However, you'll still be having a cup of coffee and talking to others. The rules of the game are the same whether the event is arranged and formal, or not arranged and informal. Networking is about using friendships, community settings, social settings, business get-togethers and industry events to promote you and your product or service.

The first rule of networking is: don't sell. I know that sounds like a strange rule, especially because we're there to sell, aren't we? Well, yes, we are there in the hope of making a sale, but obvious and too pushy selling really does put people off. Instead, be the person who doesn't just talk about himself and his product. You'll be remembered more positively for not selling, I guarantee it.

Secondly, always have your elevator speech at the ready - we'll come back to this as a separate topic - but suffice to say, this elevator speech is simply about how you describe yourself.

Thirdly, how much more you will achieve, how much more of an impression you will make, by simply talking about the other person first. In doing so, you'll be showing interest in them and creating a strong and positive impression.

Fourthly, listen actively. It's so important to actively listen. Adopt an open pose, not with your arms crossed, for example. Hold back from interrupting or contradicting. Develop a technique for remembering names so that you can use the other person's name in conversation.

Finally, when you do hit it off with someone, remember that a cup of coffee another day will be a great result. Say something along the lines of: 'It'd be useful to continue this chat when it's not so noisy. Do you mind if I give you a ring in a couple of days, so we can organise a coffee?'

Hot Tip! Treat everyone you meet as a potential opportunity to network, no matter how informal the setting. You never know…

What is this 'elevator speech' I keep hearing about?

There are generally two types of marketing message: one is short, to the point and often referred to as the elevator speech, or lift speech. It's your once-in-a-lifetime opportunity to be with someone important who asks you what you do and you only have say, thirty seconds, to make your pitch.

Imagine this. you're an entrepreneur and you're attending an event; it could be sports, social or business. At the end of the event, you decide to go to the bar or somewhere. You head over to the lifts, push the button and step through the doors of a waiting lift. Just as the doors begin to close, you hear a voice shout out, 'Hold the door!' You swing your papers or folder or bag between the closing doors and, as they open again, through the door walks someone who just happens to be an individual you could really do with getting together with.

What would you do or say? Few people are prepared to deal with such a situation. They haven't considered what they would say, much less prepared something to say or rehearsed saying it. As a result, instead of making the most of the opportunity, they just let it walk out the door. An elevator speech is a concise, carefully planned and well-practised description of you and your business that any potential customer should be able to clearly understand in the time it would take to ride up a lift or an elevator. It's the response to the question, 'What do you do?' It is not a sales pitch. Don't get caught up in using the pitch to tell the potential customer how great your product or service is.

An effective elevator speech addresses the specific interests and concerns of the person you're talking to. It needs to be conversational rather than the goal being to close the sale. The real goal of an elevator speech is just to set the hook, to catch the interest, to start a conversation with the other person.

It's also imperative that you not only prepare your elevator speech, but that you write it down and then rehearse it. There's nothing worse for you than to be thinking of what word or words to say next and to splutter and stammer. Imagine how good you'll feel, how self-confident, when you don't have to think about what to say - you just say it!

If, in response to the question, 'What do you do?' you then tell them all about your business or job, the eyes will probably glaze over and you'll lose him. However, if you happen to respond with a question, you then make the other person part of the conversation. For example, whenever I am asked the question about what I do, I always respond by saying, 'Have you ever met someone with their own business who says they need more customers?' More than likely they'll be thinking of specific people they know who've said just that. So they'll either say to me, 'Yes,' or 'Everyone wants more customers!' I can then make what I call my 'brief statement' and say, 'Well, I change the image of a small business to make them stand out from the crowd so they gain more customers and more sales.' The reaction is almost always, 'Ahhh.' Inevitably this also means that they want to know more…

How about the response to 'What do you do?' from a boiler service engineer: 'Do you know how some people worry about not having enough heat in the winter?'

Or from a painter and decorator: 'Have you ever noticed how, when you decorate your house, it's always the prep work which seems the biggest and most difficult job of all?'

The main purpose in responding with a question is that it enables more to happen rather than letting the discussion tail off into nowhere, or into polite small talk. When you get the 'Ahhh' response then you, too, have the opportunity to make your 'brief statement' about what you do. But not too much; remember that you're not here to sell.

Finally, depending on the situation and the reaction from the other party, you can end in various ways. For example:

'What's your interest at this event?' or 'What are you most wanting to get out of your visit here?' or, obviously, if you've not already asked, 'What do you do?'

The elevator speech, then, is your short marketing message. It really can be your once-in-a-lifetime opportunity, when you're with someone important who asks what you do. You'll never be stuck for words. With preparation you'll look and feel the part.

Hot Tip! Write down three questions which you might ask in response to 'What do you do?'

Hot Tip! Write down three versions of your own 'brief statement'.

Hot Tip! Practise in a mirror until you are word perfect!

Cross-selling – take an interest in your customers and let them buy more from you

When you have plenty of customers then you may not think too hard about cross-selling. What do I mean by cross-selling? Well, if you had a roadside catering trailer and sold a sandwich, cross-selling would be when you asked the customer did he want a drink as well. If you had a mechanic's garage and were completing a car service, cross-selling would be when you asked the customer, did he want a car valet as well. If you were a carpet cleaner and were finishing off a spring clean for your customer, cross-selling would be when you asked, did he want to buy some spot remover from you as well.

So, cross-selling is the simple and straightforward asking of your customers, whether they would like that little extra item; yes or no? No harm done and perhaps you could make this sort of offer in a pleasant and helpful manner. If you can, then you'll appear to be taking even more interest in your customers and their well-being.

In an easier market with plenty of customers, cross-selling opportunities can often be overlooked. However, I wonder whether you've ever heard customers say, 'I never knew you did that as well?' Maybe they've said it when you asked them how come they bought the item from a competitor!

Making clients aware of your full product range, or full range of services, will obviously serve to maximise your cross-selling opportunities. Isn't this one of the quickest ways to get more orders from your existing customers? And why not! They already know you: you already know them. They are already set up as a customer accounts perhaps. Take a genuine interest in your customers and their well-being. Perhaps they already like you if they've ordered from you before, so get them to order more items from you.

Do you remember, in the earlier chapter, my experience with the Aga service engineer? The man who never even had a brochure or business card? Well, let's be creative and think what other products he could have offered me. How about oven gloves? Anyone who has used an Aga knows that you need special long-sleeved gloves to stop being burned. How about oven cleaner, cleaning cloths, oven trays, drying rails, casserole dishes, saucepans and so on? The Aga runs on gas; how about servicing the gas fire we have as well? What about servicing the gas boiler we have? Imagine all those extra opportunities which could have been asked about but which never were. Missed forever.

Hot Tip! Set yourself the task of compiling a list of additional products and services which just might be of interest to your customers. These must complement your existing business and not make you look like a Jack-of-all-trades.

Hot Tip! From this point onwards, ask every customer without exception, 'Would you also like a …. or a ….?' Always offer alternatives: it gives your customers the power of choice.

Be the expert in your field

If you can put yourself in the position of local or regional authority in your field, then your status will grow accordingly. Your customers or potential customers will come to you, instead of you following them. How would you like it if your customers came to you? Most of us would love it!

It doesn't matter what your business or trade is; what your customers want is what you know. You and your business are paid for what you know, not for what you do. If you're a gas fitter, an electrician, a carpenter, hairdresser or bookkeeper, you already have an immense amount of knowledge that others would like to have. Most people have no idea how you do your job. At best they may know a little, a few buzz words perhaps.

For you to appear more of the expert in your field, why don't you get to know something of the history of what you do? For example, if you are a bookkeeper: the origins of a primitive double-entry system may possibly be traced as far back as the Roman Empire where the advised system was 'That the one side of the book was used for the

Debtor, the other for the Creditor.' By the end of the 15th century, the merchants in Venice certainly used the system widely. An Italian friar called Luca Pacioli, a contemporary of Leonardo da Vinci, was the first to set the system down in a mathematics textbook. He wrote down and was the first to publish a detailed description of the double-entry system which others could then study. Pacioli is often called the Father of Accounting' as a result!

Another example, if you're a gas fitter is that perhaps you should know the origins of gas as a means of light as well as heat; that there were independent suppliers of what was called 'town gas'. This was produced at the local gas works by heating up coal which then produced a gas that could be harvested. It wasn't until the 1960s that natural gas was discovered and exploited from the North Sea. And nowadays, we also actually import gas through pipelines stretching under the English Channel and the North Sea, as well as in a liquid form that's shipped to us in containers from around the world!

When you express your knowledge, whether it's as an answer to a question or even as a simple explanation or presentation, people see you as the 'all-knowing one'. You speak with authority and you become the authority. Let's face it: if the whole point is to stand out from the crowd, when you know and express your knowledge to customers - knowledge which your competitors have never bothered with - you'll stand out a mile in comparison to them.

The other thing you need to do is give your expertise away for free. Maybe you think I'm slightly mad but you can give it away free! You can get out there and demonstrate your expertise. You can show the world your knowledge. We talked in a previous chapter about press releases, in particular over the Internet. You can attend networking events where your potential customers hang out. You can show them you're an expert by offering useful solutions and advice about their problems. All these actions make you appear as an expert in your field. Your credibility will increase, your exposure will increase, and the traffic to your website will increase.

Finally, don't use the term 'expert' to describe yourself. It's nice to be referred to as an expert in something by others, but if you push this too much to promote yourself you can sound cocky. Instead, use the word 'specialist' if you need to apply a title to yourself.

Hot Tip! Try Googling the name of your trade or profession along with the words 'history of.'

Hot Tip! Prepare a one-page summary of the history of your trade or profession and try it out on your friends or family first.

Pricing – simply spell out what's so special

Why have I put pricing under this section, 'Don't die, when facing an audience'? It seemed to me a wholly and completely relevant thing to do! Any time you speak to other individuals, whether a large number at a gathering or just one individual, you'll often find yourself being asked to comment on your price or the prices in your sector. When you know clearly how you've arrived at your price then it becomes so much easier to justify it and to do so in a very confident manner indeed.

I've seen many times, with small businesses, how easy it is to slip into offering lower prices as the way to win business. The owners under-price in order to 'build up sales.' This is often the result of lack of confidence or a lack of understanding about the marketplace in which they operate. Getting your pricing right could have a huge and positive effect on your profits. How much will you charge for your service or product?

There are two methods of arriving at the price to charge: one is called cost-plus pricing; the other is called value pricing.
Using cost-plus pricing will need consideration of three elements:

- The cost to produce the goods.
- The time or labour involved.
- Your profit margin.

You'll start out by listing all the costs involved in getting your product or service to the customer, including the costs of any supplies you need to purchase and your time and labour. Using this approach can mean that some costs remain hidden, such as holiday pay, depreciation costs and maybe the costs of handling waste. There may well be others which are particular to your business. After you have worked out your costs, it is quite typical to add on your mark-up as a percentage of the cost. What mark-up might be appropriate to your particular sector is known only by you. Firstly you have to be aware of what your competitors charge. You shouldn't be wildly different from their prices, but neither should you be thinking it's necessary to charge less.

In working out costs it may be that the business owners are converting hobbies into money spinners and are simply so enthusiastic about their product that they get carried away and never really focus on making a profit. In other words, they never factor in how many hours they spend making each widget.

It may be that the business owner thinks that the path to success is to be cheaper than anyone else. This can also be the easiest way to have a business which is unsustainable. As soon as someone else comes along with a lower price they'll just be dead in the water. It's far better to focus on what else is special about a business and use the value pricing method.

Value pricing focuses not on costs but on what the customer is willing to pay. Let's face it, we don't always just buy the lowest priced product out there. We all, very often, pay a little more for some perceived added value or benefit, which we can see. What could that special thing be that you do which can offer added value? Maybe that added value is about a callout service available at differing times - certainly a plumber, for instance, can charge much more for any emergency call out and the customer will never object. Maybe the added value is about convenience – the local garage in the village miles from town can always charge a higher price for petrol or for services. Maybe the added value is more personal service – the carpet layer who shows samples at a person's home can charge more than the retail shop in town. Maybe it's about other aspects such as accessibility, a longer guarantee period, different opening hours, supply and demand and so on.

Whichever method you choose, you need to have a sound understanding of the competition. There will always be some form of competition and somebody, somewhere, will always be cheaper than you. Again, unreasonably high prices may well catch you out and any goodwill you have with your customers easily lost. Always spell out to them what it is that's special about you and the value you bring. If the customers perceive added value of some description then you can charge more than the competition, and you can justify that higher price and increase your profits accordingly.

If you're really wondering what added value you can offer, how about offering 'follow-up'? What I mean by this is to set up a process whereby you will call your customer soon after they've paid you.

I know that this sort of action is a rare event among your competitors, so promise to call and ask how the product is faring, or how the product has settled in. Ask whether any problems have occurred which you can fix? How many others do this? You can really claim some added value with this type of follow-up.

Perhaps there is something else you can do which adds value for your customers.

It's an easy thing for a new business to under price themselves in order to get a foot in the door. But the aim has to be to build up profits. Profits come when value is what's being sold.

Hot Tip! Never just quote a price all on its own and then leave it hanging. Always surround your price with benefits and with the added value you offer.

EIGHT:

What do you look like Rodney? Now let's sharpen your game even further

Websites – you might not be online, but I bet your customers are!

In these credit crunch times, people may not necessarily be spending any more money, but they are spending what they have in different ways. It used to be that people might buy goods only from a retail outlet. Nowadays they may well be searching online to find the goods, and then either order online or, as a result of their search, wander into the retail store itself. It used to be that people might have ordered from a catalogue. Well, now they may look in the catalogue but they want to know more and so check out a website for information. The fact is that the routes to market are changing, and that definitely affects you!

We often read in the newspapers about horribly expensive and botched IT blunders. An investigation by *The Independent* newspaper found that the total cost of the (Labour) government's ten most notorious IT failures was a bill for more than £26 billion for computer systems that suffered severe delays, ran way over budget or were just cancelled altogether. One of these blunders, in June 2006, was the Department For Work & Pensions benefit processing computer programme. The project was quietly scrapped after three months and little information has emerged on why it was abandoned, yet the government has admitted that £106 million had already been spent.

As a result of all these stories should you be put off anything to do with IT? No, because for your small business ***You can do it!*** Should you have a website? Definitely! Is it difficult to set one up? Definitely not! Is it expensive? You'll only pay what you want to, from just a few pounds per month to thousands a year, it all depends how sophisticated you want to be. I know plenty of tradespeople who spend maybe only £3 per month for a very credible website indeed.

Again, if your email address currently ends in such things as *virgin.net* , *aol.co.uk* , *btinternet.com* , or similar, then you can be seen as someone who just hasn't caught up yet. I don't want that to happen to you. When you buy your own website domain name, then your email address can end in your very own domain name, and not someone else's. You already look more professional.

Your website can be a simple extension of, or compilation of, all your brochures…and you don't have to pay for reprinting! You can have your website address on your business card or in an advertisement, and so much more can be offered to those looking at you, at your website.

For more sophistication and with a little more input you can even build in a shopping cart, although this may not be relevant to everyone. This may cost a little more each month but, if it suits you, then look at it this way…you aren't paying any rent for additional retail footage, are you? If you were to build in a shopping cart, then you could also automate a thank-you email to be sent out with every purchase made. On this confirmation, this thank-you, you could then add a further marketing message about another product or products. Clever, hey? Again, if customers will be able to buy from your site then use a payment method like *PayPal* because people have trust in *PayPal.*

Anyway, the Home Page is the first page they are likely to look at. There, you should have what's called a 'hero' image, that is, a top quality photo or image which conveys the impression you want people to have. This is likely to be a photo of your best work, your best service, your typical product. Alternatively, you could Google 'free images' and use some super photos available for free; just make sure the site says they are ok for commercial use. Remember that your website is your virtual shop window. It can be likened to having a retail shop but without the overheads. You can build a basic but professional-looking website in just a few hours, and there are plenty of easy to use website building tools out there.

Hot Tip! Keep it simple and do be consistent with page design; use the same layout and colour scheme for each page.

Hot Tip! Place a navigation bar on each page so that all visitors can find their way around. Include your business logo on one of the top corners of every page.

Hot Tip! Prepare, in advance, a sketch of the content for each page.

Email signatures

A signature block at the bottom of an e-mail message is a block of text which is automatically generated. It has the effect of signing off the email itself. That's all very mechanical, I know, but don't miss out on the really positive aspect to this. A good-looking signature block can help in creating your professional reputation and image: a poor signature can hurt it. In addition, you can preset different types of signature: one for new business customers, another for your regular customers, and one for friends or family.

If you get tired of typing your name and contact details over and over again at the bottom of each email then this will save you a stack of time. If you only include your name then even this will help you save some time and you'll also look the part.

Typically a signature block simply consists of one or more lines containing some brief information about you, the writer of the message. The minimum information that needs to appear will be your name, maybe your business title and your phone number along with other contact details. Including links to your website will encourage repeat visits and may attract new visitors when your email is forwarded. You could include your company logo which will again help your image. A statement is sometimes included. This may be your slogan, of course, but it's your opportunity to make that statement a good one, a professional one.

Look at the following examples to gain a picture of what the layout could be like.

George Smith
Chesterfield Florist Centre
Tel: 01162 123789 mobile: 07989 123456
website: www.floristcentre.com
Our Flowers For All Your Occasions

or,

Mary Swann
Crisp Carpet Cleaners
Te: 01601 123456 mobile: 09890 456789
website: www.marysplace.co.uk
Red Carpet Treatment For All

How to set your email signature.

It's simple, but the method can differ according to who is hosting your email account. Try going into 'Tools,' and/or 'Options,' then 'Signature,' or alternatively go to 'Help' and type in 'email signature set up.'

Hot Tip! Include your slogan as part of your email signature.

You and your appearance

'You don't get a second chance to make a first impression'

Without a shadow of doubt, this old expression is 100% true.

It's natural for every one of us to form a strong opinion of someone based on first impressions. Your appearance plays a large role in the impression you make on someone, especially on your customers. One key to successful business is always to look professional for your customers.

People who rely on face-to-face contact with clients must look the part and, when you do, the customer will feel more confident in your product and capabilities.

But what is the part you should look? Try to see things through the eyes of your customers. What do they expect? What will they notice? Your appearance sends signals to your customers about who you are and what your values are.

Certainly, if you are a builder then dress like a builder; a suit and tie might not do the trick. Then again, a polo shirt with overalls might be just what you need. A customer knows that a tradesman who takes pride in his appearance, tools and materials is likely to take pride in the job that he carries out. In a similar vein, always keep your vehicle clean in case you have to provide transport. Don't smoke in front of a customer. Do refrain from chewing gum, sniffing or swearing.

Everyone believes that personal appearance is important in succeeding at an interview and getting a job. Typically, you have twenty or thirty seconds upon meeting someone to make your first impression. Every day, people look at how we have dressed and they will judge us by the way we look. Personal appearance will play an important part in the way you are perceived and treated. Of course, every occasion we meet with a potential customer is an interview, isn't it? Be polite, always have good manners, give eye contact and a firm handshake. We pass the interview and we get the job, the quote, the tender.

Get a site survey

Most of you will have seen *The House Doctor* on television. Typically, the person selling the house is just too close to it to be objective about how it's presented for prospective customers. On TV we see the House Doctor make an on-site assessment covering a range of factors and then she shows the seller how to maximise the sales potential. Or how about *The Hotel Inspector*? Again, the owner of the guest house or hotel is just too close to it all to be able to see, to notice, what matters to the guests. The Inspector assesses physical aspects of the hotel, the surrounding areas and competitors. She then makes specific recommendations to the owner to make the place so much more appealing.

In your own business you are probably too close to see that what might be an eyesore to customers, is something that you have become used to over a period of time. Think about getting a site survey from a totally independent, third party. This is a task which a marketing consultant could do for you. You'll get an assessment of how your business stands up in the local marketplace, especially in comparison to your competitors. You should then end up with a report on marketing tactics which can help to pull customers in; on recommendations about how you might stand out from the crowd; on enhancements to your operation; service and product ideas to help you grow; and an action plan based on the assessment.

When you work somewhere day in and day out, it's so easy not to notice what a first-time customer might notice. It's usually the simple things, too, like layout or presentation. Obviously the benefits of having someone else look at your business with a fresh pair of eyes can be numerous. They may see things which you had never considered. What have you got to lose? What might you gain?

Hot Tip! Get a completely independent comment from a third party. Get them to look at your business through the eyes of a customer and then give you feedback.

Small exhibitions can be big opportunities

Before you say exhibitions are not for you, let's just think this topic through. Attendance at a full blown business exhibition at Earls

Court or the NEC is not what I'm suggesting and you're correct, it definitely may not be right for you. However, there are many other opportunities available for you to show your product or services, and when you do exhibit it gives you the chance to talk to other people who are your prospective customers. Why is this so important? It's so important for this reason - people buy from people and that's a fact! Besides, we all want to feel a product, to squeeze it and poke it, to understand it before we buy. We also want to meet and speak to the person behind the product or the service. For you it gives the chance to demonstrate what you do; the chance to ask and answer questions; to build good customer relationships. In fact, where else could you go to meet, face to face, so many possible customers in a day as at some kind of exhibition?

Again, any customers to your table or stall or stand, are likely to be more receptive because they've come to the event by choice.

So, if it's not the NEC or Earls Court, where else can you exhibit which won't cost an arm and a leg? Answer? Lots of places and I'll list them: local authority events, church fetes, school events, village hall events, craft fairs, wedding fairs, themed events, sponsored events, grand openings, car boot sales, fun days, Christmas fairs, coffee mornings, Fair Trade events, garden shows, sporting events.

Follow what your local newspaper columns mention under *What's on?* or look on websites that list events in your area to see what there is coming up in the near future. Small exhibitions really can be big opportunities.

What do you need as a minimum? Well, any flyers or leaflets you have. Certainly come armed with your business cards. If you have any product cards bring these too and don't forget to bring your smile! What might be nice but which you don't have to have, would be a table covering or any signage available, plus any giveaways you have with your name and number on.

Hot Tip! Make sure your name is printed in the event programme.

Hot Tip! Arrange for the event website to be linked to your website and put your stand details on your website.

Hot Tip! Let your customers know you'll be there and perhaps invite some of them.

Offer a guarantee and make your customers feel at ease

Too many guarantees are watered down, diluted. Do you want your customers to be completely certain that they're buying from the right person? Do you want them to come back, confidently, and make repeat purchases from you? Of course you do; so provide a full guarantee to them.

One of the most common reasons why people won't buy from you is that they see some kind of risk in purchasing your product or service. They're worried that they might be making the wrong decision. One of the very best ways for you to overcome this concern is to offer a guarantee which will either take the risk out for the customers entirely, or reduce it so substantially, that the customers are now totally at ease as a result. Removing any risk, while your competitors do not, will go a long way to making you stand out from the crowd. Providing a full guarantee on your work can result in you attracting business which otherwise would have gone to a competitor. The occasional refund here and there will definitely be a demonstration of your good faith towards your customers. If you take a lot of pride in what you do then why not offer a 'no quibble' guarantee for them? You're much more likely to end up with more sales and more profits as a result - and just think of the positive aspects this will raise for your reputation?

Hot Tip! Remember: the customer is always right even when he's wrong.

Your complete marketing message

In a previous chapter we spoke about how there are generally two types of marketing message. The first one is short, to the point and usually referred to as your elevator speech. That's your once-in-a-lifetime opportunity, when you only have, say, thirty seconds to make your pitch.

The second type is the complete marketing message, and you should definitely spend enough time to develop this type of message clearly.

Taking time to prepare and write out your complete marketing message will reap tremendous benefits for you later. Can you do this yourself? Yes, ***You can do it!*** Simply go through the exercise of answering the following questions.

1. What are your customer's problems? Can you write them down?

2. How can you convey a sense of urgency, what might happen if they're not dealt with swiftly?
3. Why is your business the one to solve this problem?
4. What are the benefits of the solution that you will provide?
5. What about your 'no quibble' guarantee? [Include it here.]

In addition, consider how

6. We've already discussed the power of testimonials. This is the perfect place for you to use any of them.
7. Be clear about any prices and charges.

This exercise will force you to sit and consider your business, consider the marketplace and consider your customers. It's a good exercise for you because when you set down the answers in writing, you will have a much fuller understanding of what you are doing with your business. Your confidence will grow and your knowledge will increase. You can then make decisions about how best to communicate your complete marketing message to your customers.

When you have compiled your complete marketing message, then identify every platform where it's going to be used: in your brochures; on your website; use selected parts for any press releases; use selected parts in your local adverts; use part of it when networking.

Hot Tip! Systematically work through the seven questions/reminders listed above and write out your own complete marketing message.

Hot Tip! Make use of the template I've included in the Appendix, entitled 'Marketing Plan'. By filling this in, you'll be able to complete a year-long plan to help join together all the items we have covered in this book.

The Beginning!

At the start of this book I quoted Harvard Business School's definition of *marketing* as 'all the things you do to make the telephone ring.' They also defined *selling* as 'all the things you do after you pick up the telephone.' Well, when you've put your plan for marketing together, that really is the beginning for you: everything else follows on from there. It's of no use your putting all of my suggestions into practice, if you don't recognize this point as being the start of everything else. Selling will now start.

Selling isn't nearly so complex as marketing and the difference between success and failure can be one simple word: 'Yes.'

Some people think that to be successful in selling you need the gift of the gab. Well, that just isn't so. Some think that you need to be hard-faced about it all; that couldn't be further from the truth either. None of us responds very well to those who talk us to death or are too pushy. It's not what we want. The most successful salespeople I know are well mannered, polite individuals who I'd say do not sell: they simply help people to buy! They build trust by asking gentle questions and listening carefully to the answers. And, ***You can do it*** too.

The secret to success in sales? Asking the right questions in the right manner, listening to the answers and watching for those all important buying signals. ***You can do it.*** Keep your eyes open for my next book, about selling. It will be the beginning of a new experience for you.

Appendix I

Sample template: Customer Testimonial Form

Company Name / Logo
CUSTOMER TESTIMONIAL We really do appreciate your support. You've recently had some work carried out by us and we'd very much like to capture a few comments about your experience. Please do answer the following questions in your own words.
Customer Name:
What did you need or what was the situation that brought you to our business?
What did you get from us / what was your initial experience?
Are there any special comments you'd like to pass on?
May I quote you on future marketing materials?
Thank you so much for your time!

Appendix II

Sample template: Customer Feedback Questionnaire

Company Name / Logo
CUSTOMER FEEDBACK QUESTIONNAIRE We'd really like your feedback please. You've just had some work carried out by us and to help improve our services could you answer the questions below?
Customer Name:
Nature of Work Carried Out:
Your views: Please rate the following:
Poor - Below Avg – Avg – Good – Exc
Response to initial enquiry Quality of service Tidiness Reliability/timekeeping Courtesy Quality of Workmanship Value for money
How else can we improve our service? Are there any additional products or services you think we should have?
Thank you for your time!

Appendix III

Sample template: Press Release Form

Company Name / Logo
PRESS RELEASE **Date of Issue:** dd/mm/yyyy **For Immediate Release** **HEADLINE** - make it short and sweet! (clear and simple is the watchword of the day & keep it to just one line)
SUBHEADING – (This gives you a chance to add just a little to the headline. You can use this to alert journalists to a specific date, event or location).
BODY – (Your first sentence will be a summary of the story. The rest of the opening paragraph will be the what, where, when, who and why. In the second paragraph, explain what is so special or unique about your story. Use any subsequent paragraphs to support opinions or claims with facts and figures. Do try to highlight your story with quotes from your customers or key individuals. Ensure your press release is no more than two pages).
For more information please contact: Your name Your telephone number Your email address
'Notes To Editors' Include here a quick background on your business. State here whether you have photos available. Include here a reference to your website if you have one. 'Notes To Editors' is the ideal place to explain any technical or difficult bits of information mentioned in the Body.
ENDS (gives the clearest indicator that there is no more to follow).

Appendix IV

Sample template: Marketing Plan Form

ABC COMPANY MARKETING PLAN FOR YEAR yyyy/yyyy
MARKETING OBJECTIVES: (include any objectives, such as increasing customers, selling more to current customers, keeping more customers etc.)
CUSTOMERS: include a description of your customers, their profile and where they are to be found.)
YOUR CUSTOMERS PROBLEMS: (include the issues and problems your customers face and write down your solution to these problems.)
YOUR COMPETITION: (list all current competitors and state how they try to solve the customers' problems.)
WHAT MAKES YOU SO DIFFERENT?: (include what it is about you and your business that makes you stand out from other competitors.)
MARKETING CALENDAR: (include all activities that apply.) **QUARTERLY-** **MONTHLY-** **WEEKLY-** **ONGOING-**
MARKETING BUDGET: (list the costs of all activities and record in each month of your financial plans.)

About the author

Allan Rimmer is a successful entrepreneur, consultant, business speaker and workshop provider. After a career in sales, sales management and sales training, Allan found an opportunity to start his own business. With a small bank loan, a low-cost, weekly rented office, two second hand desks and telephones for him and his wife Stephanie, away he went in the business services' sector. Overheads were ruthlessly scrutinised and it wasn't until year two that their first employee was taken on. Allan knows about low-cost marketing as a direct result of his own personal experiences.

Some years later, with fifty plus employees and annual sales of £8.25 million, a trade sale of the business was completed. Moving onwards and upwards from that sale to providing consulting services, Allan has since worked with a wide variety of businesses. He has delivered workshops and seminars to numerous entrepreneurs and individuals wanting to understand how to start a new business, or how to grow an existing business.

It was during this latter period that Allan heard repeated many times the words, 'I've got the business idea; now I just need to get the customers!' Allan realised that there was a very real need and demand to know the basics of marketing in order to attract more customers. He also realised that this acquisition of knowledge had to be matched to low-cost solutions. The budgets for marketing expenditure are simply not available to small entrepreneurs. Thus, the idea for writing a book on low-cost marketing solutions was born.

Visit his website at www.plainspkg.co.uk.

www.ingramcontent.com/pod-product-compliance
Ingram Content Group UK Ltd.
Pitfield, Milton Keynes, MK11 3LW, UK
UKHW041922190726
13854UKWH00003B/1395